SPIRIT OF

WELLS
CATHEDRAL

ROBERT DUNNING

images by Michael Blandford

First published in Great Britain in 2009

British Library Cataloguing-in-Publication Data
A CIP record for this title is available from the British Library

ISBN 978 1 906887 36 0

PiXZ Books
Halsgrove House, Ryelands Industrial Estate,
Bagley Road, Wellington, Somerset TA21 9PZ
Tel: 01823 653777
Fax: 01823 216796
email: sales@halsgrove.com

An imprint of Halstar Ltd, part of the Halsgrove group of companies
Information on all Halsgrove titles is available at: www.halsgrove.com

Printed and bound by Grafiche Flaminia, Italy

Introduction

The Resurrection
and an angel

The Spirit of Wells Cathedral is so powerful and compelling that people come here again and again. The building has a unity and a scale that make it both satisfying and familiar, and the site beside the springs that explain its name is exquisite. Yet those who know the building well still see things they had never noticed before. In style pure Gothic, pure English, its magic is revealed by sunlight streaming in at different angles according to the season and the time of day; by candlelight when the sun has set and, in recent years, by the many facets of artificial light. Light, music and the cathedral's story were brought together in a dazzling performance for Annie Maw, the High Sheriff of Somerset, in September 2007 and were the inspiration for this book that seeks to share the Spirit of Wells Cathedral with a wider audience.

Left: Unity and scale: the vaulted nave

Right: The wells of St Andrew

Sunlight in the South Quire Aisle

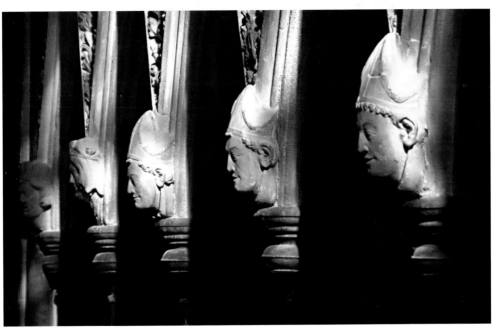

Watchers in the Chapter House

Lighting the Triforium at
Christmas

Right: Christmas Concert

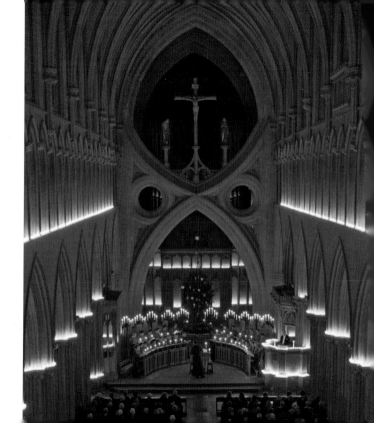

The story of Wells Cathedral begins where water from the Mendips bubbles to the surface, a spot cherished at least since Roman times. Ina, king of the West Saxons, built a church here very early in the eighth century to serve as a minster, a centre of mission for the expanding Christian Faith among the still pagan Saxon settlers. In 909 its clergy were joined by Athelm, the first bishop of Wells, and he and his successors set up their teaching stool (cathedra) there. From about 1090 the bishops made the abbey at Bath their cathedral, but clergy at Wells continued their work, growing so influential that in about 1175 Bishop Reginald de Bohun (or FitzJocelin) decided to rebuild their church. When enough of the new building was ready the clergy brought from the old minster their most precious possessions, among them the bones of previous bishops of Wells, their massive cope chest and their font; that font they placed in the new south transept, as close to the old church as was convenient.

The wells from the Camery

Bishop Giso, removed from the old cathedral

The grave of the Founder, King Ina

Left: The Saxon font

The cope chest

Bishop Reginald's church was original in style and designed by a brilliant master mason whose name has not survived. Its building took only about 65 years, beginning at the east end. When work had reached part way down the nave it stopped abruptly because the whole country was placed under Interdict and all church building and worship ceased in 1208-9 until the quarrel between King John and the Pope was healed. When work began again Bishop Jocelin, a native of Wells, who had already built a house that would become part of the Palace, was in office and a new master mason, Adam Lock, was in charge of work. Adam did not live to see the cathedral finished: the highly-coloured west front was completed by his successor Thomas Norreys and Bishop Jocelin blessed the completed work in 1239.

Simplicity and elegance enclosing the ornate clock

Bishop Jocelin's undercroft welcomes visitors to the Palace

Adam Lock, Master Mason

The vault of Adam Lock's nave

A thorn in the flesh

Left: Grape stealers

For some fifty years from about 1290 a second building campaign transformed the eastern end of the cathedral. Bishop William de Marchia's name is linked with the completion of the Chapter House; Bishop Walter Haselshaw (archdeacon, dean and then bishop between 1286 and 1308) must have been intimately involved with the new Lady Chapel (needed because of new and elaborate forms of worship). Bishops John Droxford (1309-29) and Ralph of Shrewsbury (1329-63) actively supported deans Henry Husee and John de Godeley, and their master masons Thomas of Witney and William Joy with money not only to build the Lady Chapel and its link with the older Quire (Retrochoir), to remodel the central tower and to deal with the almost disastrous consequences – strengthening its base first with additional masonry in its surrounding supports and then by building the famous 'scissor' arches.

The Lady Chapel

Left: The great West Front

The Lady Chapel vault

The Chapter House

Bishop John Droxford

Left: Outside the Chapter House

The scissor arches

Bishop Ralph of Shrewsbury was bishop here during the Black Death, but just before its outbreak he had completed (on a narrow plot beside one of the clergy houses next to the cathedral) two lines of small houses, a chapel and a hall for the use of those cathedral clergy (called Vicars Choral) who led the singing of the regular services. Even earlier, perhaps in anticipation of the visit of Edward III, he must have spent a huge sum of money on the official home of the bishops on the south side of the cathedral: a moat was dug around the buildings of Bishops Jocelin and Robert Burnell and walls and towers built. From that time it was known as a palace. Bishop Ralph escaped the plague by living far away in his manor house at Wiveliscombe.

The Vicars' chapel

Bishop Ralph of Shrewsbury

Right: A glimpse into the Vicars' Close

The Vicars' Hall

The Bishop's Palace

Bishop Ralph's moat

Nicholas Bubwith (bishop 1407-24) served both Richard II and Henry IV, the latter as secretary, chaplain, Keeper of the Rolls of Chancery (government records), Keeper of the Privy Seal and briefly Treasurer of England. His many rewards included several archdeaconries and within a year from 1406 held three bishoprics in turn, London, Salisbury and Wells. He was still in government service for several years after coming here as bishop, and for nearly four years was out of England as leader of the English delegation to the reforming Council at Constance. In his long will he made clear his great concern for his cathedral by leaving money: for a north-west tower, as far as possible like that paid for by Bishop John Harewell; enough to rebuild the eastern arm of the cloister with a library above (designed by a mason from Gloucester); and yet more to create a chapel to hold his remains, where three priests would regularly pray for his soul.

Bishop Bubwith's holly leaves
in a library window

The west towers: Harewell's on right, Bubwith's on left

Bishop Bubwith's library above East Cloister

The Bubwith chapel

Top right: The library with seventeenth-century furnishings

Right: The Reading Room

Thomas Bekynton (bishop 1443-65) came to Wells as bishop after serving as royal secretary and diplomat, and was here during the early years of the Wars of the Roses. He was a scholar from a humble background and a generous patron to promising young scholars. He organised his tomb and chapel in 1451-2, well before his death, as a daily reminder of the uncertainty of life. He gave money to build the famous gatehouses – the Bishop's Eye leading to the Palace, the Penniless Porch and Brown's Gate guarding the Cathedral Green, and the Chain Gate, not simply another entrance but also a bridge to be used by the Vicars Choral going between their homes and the cathedral. In the Penniless Porch and behind the Bishop's Eye is the bishop's rebus, his badge, a beacon made from a flaming barrel (tun) on a pole. Only part of his contribution to the Bishop's Palace survives: a cloister was pulled down long ago, but in the present bishop's house is a tower, the tall ground-floor room used as a chapel and in 1456 called the 'new oratory'. Part of its painted decoration has been found hidden under floorboards in the room above.

Bishop Thomas Bekynton

The robed bishop
above his skeleton

The vaulting of
Bekynton's chapel

Penniless Porch and Bishop's Eye: market day

Bekynton's
beacon and tun

Chain Gate, a bridge for the Vicars Choral

The tower of the
Bishop's Palace

Hugh Sugar, one of Bishop Bekynton's promising young scholars, a doctor of laws and a clergyman, came from Romsey. He worked in this diocese for nearly 40 years and from 1460 until his death in 1489 was the domineering Treasurer of the cathedral. He was also the leading lawyer in the diocese and was the senior judge in its courts. Near the end of his life he quarrelled with most of the cathedral clergy about burials there and about cutting down or pruning the trees on Cathedral Green. Any formal appeal they made against him was impossible because he had one of the keys to the chest where the cathedral's seal was kept. After his death his executors were allowed to build a chapel now named after him that has carvings including doctor's caps and sugar loaves. Such bad behaviour would have been unlikely had Dean John Gunthorpe not been away serving kings Edward IV and Richard III, though the dean employed William Smyth, the cathedral master mason, to rebuild his house (now the Old Deanery) and perhaps later to enlarge it when Henry VII came to visit in 1491.

Sugar's doctor's
cap and sugar loaves

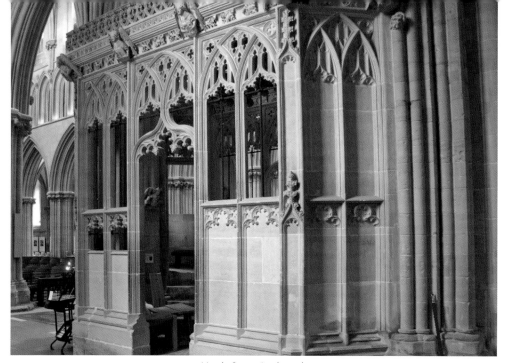

Hugh Sugar's chapel

Empty niches in Sugar's chapel

Dean Gunthorpe's house

William Knight (bishop 1541-7) was a Londoner and a career diplomat who came to Wells when religion was becoming political and he died nine months after Henry VIII when radicals were taking control of government and public preaching was becoming popular. He himself seems to have been a religious traditionalist but had worked in Italy where the revival of Classical art was widespread, and he wished to have a pulpit for his tomb. It seems a sort of compromise: its wooden sounding board (now a table in Dunster Castle) bears a text in Latin; the text in stone is in English, one word changed from the first English Bible of 1539 to the Authorized Version of 1611. And another change came later and is a puzzle. The bishop's coat of arms, clear from a nearby window, has been changed: a double-headed eagle has become something much more like a whale! Who did that, and why?

The bishop's coat of arms in glass

Bishop Knight's pulpit

The altered text: REPR[OVE] for IMP[ROVE]

Another alteration

Bishops in the past were not especially interested in music at Wells; that was the concern of the cathedral's governing body, the Dean and Chapter. The king and bishop and those curious stone brackets jutting out from the wall high up on the south side of the nave mark the position of the first known organ (however difficult for the organist to reach). Later organs, like the present one, stood on the pulpitum or screen between and were sometimes described as two organs, one facing west, the other east. One organ, built in 1620 for nearly £400, suffered a dreadful fate when it was broken down by Parliamentary soldiers in the Civil War. It remained silent for a time but was patched up when the bishop and the dean returned from exile in 1660. Two years later Robert Taunton of Bristol was asked to build a new one for no more than £800, and Bishop William Piers gave the dean £50 for

Quire embroideries

the old one. The new one was painted white and gold and included carvings of St Andrew and cherubs. Troops came again to Wells in 1685 and were said to have 'almost' ruined it; the 'almost' seems to have meant that they were persuaded to leave it alone, for no money was spent on it for nearly a century. The present organ, in a case designed by Alan Rome in 1974, is the result of several modifications and repairs since the 17th century.

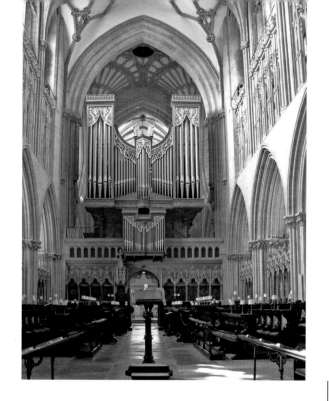

Left: King and bishop near to the first organ

Right: Organ and Quire

'The control panel'

The choir in action

Choir seats and canons' stalls

The Spirit of Wells Cathedral comes obviously from the building, but also from the nearly nine hundred years of regular services held in it and from the relationships of bishops, deans and others who have worked here. Restoration of the fabric was undertaken seriously in the nineteenth century and again in the twentieth, the repair of the West Front calling for a huge international effort led by Dean Patrick Mitchell. The return to colourful styles of worship was particularly marked by the reintroduction of the figures of the Rood above the scissor arches by Dean Armitage Robinson. Altar and furnishings in the nave are the particular contributions of the late twentieth century, shown off to great effect by the colourful and exquisite altar frontals and vestments. They and the significant new buildings for music, education, restaurant and shop and the adaptation of the undercroft of the Chapter House as an exhibition space are the particular contribution of Dean Richard Lewis and his successor Dean John Clarke supported by a hugely loyal staff and the financial support of an astounding number of people. The Spirit of Wells Cathedral is alive and moving.

Two restored figures in the West Front galaxy

The restored Rood

Nave altar at Advent with clergy seat and choir stalls

High altar at Easter

Cope inspired by vaulting

Friends Building
education room

Louis the cathedral cat is alive but not always moving; appearing without warning in unlikely and often inconvenient places; unpredictable as any cat, entirely his own person. A Spirit at large in this most spiritual cathedral.

Louis the heat-seeker

Light and shadow in the nave

Right: The Chapter House steps

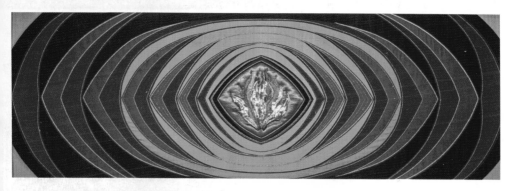

Pentecost altar frontals

The Crucified Christ